AMANDA DOBRA HOPE

I Want You to Know

Words of Inspiration for Young People

First published by Golden Dolphin Publishing 2021

Copyright © 2021 by Amanda Dobra Hope

All rights reserved. No part of this publication may be reproduced, stored, transmitted in any form or by any means, electronic, mechanical, photocopying, recording, scanning, or otherwise without written permission from the publisher. It is illegal to copy this book, post it to a website, or distribute it by any other means without permission.

First edition

ISBN: 978-0-578-31074-9

Cover art by: Amanda Dobra Hope

Your parents are here to guide you, not to think for you.

All of your thoughts and choices are yours alone.

You are *worthy* of happy feelings and emotions.

You are special in your own unique way.

Always be true to that.

Do not conform when it is against your core being.

You are a blessing to the world.

What you chose to do in life will affect so many others along your path.

Listen quietly to your inner voice every day.

See what it has to say to you about your path to personal satisfaction and purpose in the world.

Remember that we are all connected, and no one has all of the answers.

All of us are trying to find our own way, from the smallest child to the oldest adult.

Although it may be hard,
there are times when
you may feel all alone in
your beliefs.

Gather your courage and
believe anyway, even if
silently for awhile.

Remember that the people you admire have quiet struggles of their own.

No one is free from life's continual lessons.

Their lessons are just different than yours.

Be true to yourself.

No one knows what is best for you better than you.

Remember that any advice you are given may be well intended, but may also have nothing to do with you.

It may simply be the personal experience of the person giving the advice.

Listen to all, but do not follow blindly.

You are with yourself 24 hours a day, and only you know your entire situation.

Consider that those who continuously offer advice will have to go back to worrying about how to live their own life when they're done acting like they know how to live yours.

There is opportunity around every corner.

Be willing to recognize and act upon it when it shows up, but don't force things that aren't ready yet.

They will come.

You may need to open or close a few more doors first.

Be willing to ask your higher power (however you understand it) for help when you need it.

Then go about your life, but with eyes wide open, able to recognize the help when it comes through.

The better you feel about yourself and your beliefs, no matter what anyone says to you, the more you will attract those who feel the same.

Do not give up.

Even if you feel like the strangest person in the world who will never fit in, there are others like you.

They may not have emerged from their silence yet.

Your heart, brain, and spirit are no different than that of any other great thinker, politician, humanitarian, performer, or athlete.

Everyone needs to live out their contribution to the world in their own unique way.

Slow down! Society has driven itself into a stressed-out frenzy.

We can change this collective feeling if we no longer see value in the frenzy and refuse to buy in.

We will find other ways to survive.

It wasn't always like this.

Take everyone you meet with a grain of salt.

There will be great life teachers for you all throughout your life.

You have something to learn from them, but they have things to learn from you as well.

Remember that no one has all of the answers.

Accept their guidance graciously and gratefully, but do not idolize them as "all knowing."

Remember that your beliefs and truths apply to your life.

Be true to yourself, but do not force others to believe in or follow your truths.

Remember that you were born for a reason.

Nothing happens by accident, and your life has a purpose and gift for this world.

Live with integrity.

Do not cause intentional harm, sadness, or loss to others—even if they have hurt you.

There is no other way to
break the cycle of greed,
hurt, helplessness, and lost
hope than with love.

Love yourself and others,
despite all of our shortcomings.

Similarly, do not
subject yourself to harm.

If you are able to get away safely
from a dangerous
(to your mind or body)
situation, get away.

If not, use all of your power
to project forgiveness
and blessings on those
that are hurting you, and
wish for their own hearts
to be healed with love.

Remember when you fall or think you have failed, you have not.

You are going through the situation to better prepare yourself for something greater.

No bad days, joyous days, or "nothing" days are ever without purpose.

All of them have a purpose in your greater plan.

Hold gratitude in your heart for at least a few minutes every day.

Even if life seems to be its darkest, you can always find something to be grateful for.

This gratitude will always flow back to you in some way.

Above all, be true to yourself, because without the real you, we are all missing one of
life's greatest gifts.

All of this and more
I *wish* for you.

Have a spectacular life,
and a grand adventure!

About the Author

Amanda Dobra Hope, D.Hlc (Doctor of Holistic Life Coaching), M. Div., is an evolutionary teacher, award-winning author, speaker (TEDx, conferences, summits, etc.), vision-holder, and holistic life coach.

The author of: The Healing of the Masculine and Feminine- How to Truly Change the World From the Inside, Out; Holding Space-A Guide to Supporting Others While Remembering to Take Care of Yourself First; and Life Salad- Everyday Keys to Finding and Living Your Inner Truth, Amanda's passion lies in helping people to develop healthier relationships with themselves—leading to healthier relationships with those around them, and in turn, the world as a whole.

She empowers people to discover their authentic self and then to create a life in alignment with it. Amanda excels at meeting people where they are at, holding them safe, and showing them where their true brilliance lies. Her sense of humor and warm personality allow her to quickly and deeply connect with readers, audiences, and clients. She is passionate about helping others uncover their true inner selves so that all have a chance to give their unique gifts in a world that works for everyone. Her belief is that when everyone on the planet loves themselves and can express their true gifts with passion and authenticity, we will all thrive. Find her at www.itsasyoulikeit.com

www.ingramcontent.com/pod-product-compliance
Lightning Source LLC
Chambersburg PA
CBHW071845290426
44109CB00017B/1934